alphabetics

/ an aesthetically awesome
alliterated alphabet anthology

/ written by patrick & traci concepción
illustrated by dawid ryski

LITTLE
GESTALTEN

/ for Juliet

Aa

/ Atticus the altruistic astronaut
admires an ascending apple
while aviating through an anti-gravity abyss

Bb

/ Butch the boisterous black bear
bears a baby blue blazer, bowtie, and boat shoes
while balancing on his buddy bicycle
believing to be a bird

Cc

/ Colossal Cornelius
captures curious carnie companions
on his classic Contaflex camera

Dd

/ Daisy the dauntless diver
dares a death-defying dip in the Danube
with dangersome dinosaurs

Ee

/ Ezra the eccentric eskimo
embarks on an expedition to Everest
on his earmuff wearing elephant

Ff

/ fuddled Franz
fancies flannels and feathers
while foraging flamboyant foxes in the forest

Gg

/ Gus the gregarious giant
with geek chic glasses
and garb gathered from Goodwill
gambols on his Gibson guitar

Hh

/ hellion Harlow and her honey Hans
hum the holiday highway heat
on her hellacious Harley hog

/ Ivan and Iver
the identical indigenous Iroquis
ice skate idyllic Idlewild Lake

Jj

/ Jovial jetsetters Jackie and Jolene
jubilantly jitterbug in Johannesburg
to a jamboree of jazz jingles

Kk

/ Kingston the kickboxing kangaroo
wears knee high socks
while knocking out an off-key karaoke crooner

Ll

/ Leon the lucha libre legend
in his lucky leotard
is lavishly loved by Latin locals

Mm

/ motion picture maker Maximo
meanders on his marvellous moped
mindfully maneuvering his movie camera

Nn

/ Neville the nautical nomad
with a Norwegian neckbeard
navigates nonstop on a native narwhal

Oo

/ Orson the omnipotent octopus
of the open ocean
overpowers an offensive oil tanker

Pp

/ Paris the pretentious peacock
puffs on a Peterson pipe
while perched upon a penny-farthing

Qq

/ Quinn the quail queen
quietly queued for the
quintessential quinoa quiche

Rr

/ Roxanne the rambunctious raccoon
rocks out on a reel-to-reel recorder
resonating rambling rockabilly

Ss

/ Stella the sultry seafaring sailor
sails south on her schooner
seeking the seldom seen Siamese sperm whale
with her spyglass

Tt

/ Thelonious the tattooed thief
takes his three-legged terrier
on a treadmill toddle

Uu

/ Uma the unpredictable unicorn
underneath an ultraviolet umbrella
unleashes her unicycle in an über upscale uptown

Vv

/ Virgil the vampire
(v)wears a velvet vest
(v)while vexed on (v)which vintage vinyl
to play on his Victor-Victrola

Ww

/ wanderlust Wren with a walrus mustache
enjoys wearing a warbonnet and warpaint
while wayfaring with warbling whales

Xx

/ Xander the extravagant Texan
exhibits his T-rex through an exposing x-ray
to an exhilarated influx of folks

Yy

/ Yvette the yuppie Yeti
yodels a yearnful yawn
after finishing a yard of fro yo in the Yukon

Zz

/ Zooey the zonked zombie
gazes at zany zeppelins
with Zig-Zags in Zürich

Glossary

altruistic / selfless, concerned for the well-being of others

ascending / moving upwards

boisterous / expressing exuberance and happiness

carnie / slang term used for a carnival worker

colossal / a person or thing of immense size or power

Contaflex / a type of camera popularized in the 1930s - 60s

dauntless / showing fearlessness and determination

eccentric / deviating from convention in a bizarre manner, irregular or odd

flamboyant / strikingly bold or colorful, showy

foraging / searching for food or provisions

fro yo / short for frozen yogurt

fuddled / confused

gambol / to leap about playfully, frolic

garb / a distinctive style or form of clothing

gregarious / seeking and enjoying the company of others

hellacious / exceptionally powerful

hellion / a troublesome or mischievous person

idyllic / peaceful or picturesque

indigenous / native, local

jamboree / a large, festive gathering with music and dancing

jitterbug / an exuberant early 20th century dance

jovial / cheerful and friendly

jetsetters / people who travel from one fabulous place to another

lavishly / giving in great amounts

lucha libre / a form of freestyle wrestling originating in Mexico

meander / a winding path or course

moped / a low-power, lightweight motorized bicycle

narwahl / a small Arctic whale that has one long twisted tusk

nautical / concerning sailors or navigation

neckbeard / facial hair existing on the neck

nomad / a person who travels from place to place with no permanent home

omnipotent / having unlimited power

penny-farthing / a type of bicycle with a large front wheel and a much smaller rear wheel

Peterson pipe / an Irish brand of tobacco pipes developed by Charles Peterson

pretentious / expressing exaggerated worth or stature in an attepmt to impress others

queue / to take one's place in line

quinoa / a delicious grain with a lot of protein, traditionally grown in South America

quiche / a pielike dish usually containing egg, cheese and vegetables

quintessential / representing the most perfect example of something

rambling / moving without any clear purpose or direction

rambunctious / difficult to control in a way that is playfull or full of energy

reel-to-reel / recording equipment in which the tape passes between two mounted reels

resonating / producing a strong deep tone

rockabilly / a type of music that combines elements of rock and roll and country music

schooner / a type of sailboat with two or more masts

seafaring / using the sea for travel or transportation

sultry / attractive in a way that suggests a passionate nature

toddle / to walk with short, unsteady steps

über / indicating an outstanding or supreme example of a particular kind of person or thing

vexed / bothered or worried

Victor-Victrola / early 20th century company that manufactured phonographs

wanderlust / a strong desire to travel

wayfaring / traveling

yearnful / nostagically or wistfully longing for something

yuppie / a young, well-paid, middle-class professional who has a luxurious lifestyle

zeppelin / a large flying airship that is long and cylindrical in shape with a rigid framework

Zig-Zag / a French brand of rolling papers

zonk / to fall suddenly and heavily asleep

Imprint

Alphabetics
An Aesthetically Awesome Alliterated Alphabet Anthology

Written by Patrick & Traci Concepción
Illustrated by Dawid Ryski
Typeface: Helvetica Neue by Linotype

Printed by Livonia Print, Riga
Made in Europe

Published by Little Gestalten, Berlin 2014
ISBN: 978-3-89955-728-2

2nd printing, 2015

For more information, please visit little.gestalten.com.

Bibliographic information published by the Deutsche Nationalbibliothek.
The Deutsche Nationalbibliothek lists this publication in the Deutsche Nationalbibliografie; detailed bibliographic data are available online at http://dnb.d-nb.de.

This book was printed on paper certified by the FSC®.

Acknowledgements

Juliet / our beautiful daughter

Anula and Frank / Dawid's loves

Pedro and Loubelle; Jeff and Elaine / our loving parents, supportive of all of the crazy
ideas we've had over the years

Tina and Antonio; Kyle, Audrey and Cameron / our sisters, brothers and nephew who make
life even more beautiful

Toto / the most selfless person on the planet

Members Only / the greatest assemblage of people, ever

The Playaz / best friends for life

The Schaeffers / best neighbors ever

Mark and Amanda / insightful friends

Carl / our best friend and Roomba

Bob, Johnny, LeVar, Mr. Torquemada, Dexter Building 34, Gordo, Helvetica Neue